This is a Grandreams Book
This edition published in 2004

Grandreams Books Ltd
4 North Parade, Bath BA1 1LF, UK

Designed and packaged by
Q2A Design Studio

Printed in China

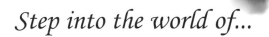

Step into the world of...

The
Vikings

Contents

The Viking Age

Over 1000 years ago, a group of people from the Scandinavian countries of Denmark, Sweden and Norway began to explore the world. They were not just explorers but mighty warriors who travelled the seas and invaded foreign lands. They were the Vikings, who ravaged many lands to find riches, slaves and homes to live in.

In Search of Home...

The Vikings found life difficult at home because of poor farmland and harsh weather conditions. Slowly, they started to sail to other countries in search of easier living.

Ravens Flying High!

The most famous Viking Age symbol is the raven banner. Although most people believe that it was the Viking national flag, it was supposedly carried by one particular leader. It was a triangular banner featuring a black raven. Legend has it that Viking sailors carried the bird with them to sea. They would then set it free and it would lead them to the nearest land, safety or victory!

The Viking raven banner was probably the first flag to fly over North America, when Leif Ericsson carried it to Newfoundland for good luck

The Viking Age

How long did the Viking Age last?

The Viking Age began over 1000 years ago and lasted for more than 300 years. It came to an end at the Battle of Hastings in 1066, with the introduction of Christianity in Scandinavia. By then, most European states had also become capable of defending themselves against Viking raiders.

What does the term 'Viking' mean?

The word 'Viking' is said to have originated from the Old Norse word, *vikingr* or *vikinger*, meaning 'sea raider' or 'pirate'. The term has also been said to mean 'one who lurks in a *vik* (Old Norse for creek or inlet)'.

The Thing was a platform for Viking freemen to make decisions on laws and punishments for criminals. It was also held to elect chieftains and kings

How do we know so much about the Vikings?

We know all about the Vikings because of the *Icelandic Sagas*. These are the 1000-year-old manuscripts that record the lives and achievements of powerful Viking kings and rulers. We also know about the Viking Age thanks to archaeologists who found old Viking artefacts and settlements.

What kind of government did the Vikings have?

At first, the Vikings did not have proper kings and empires. Denmark was the only Viking country with a king, but he did not rule over the entire country. Kings were helped by nobles and decisions were made at assemblies called Things. A Thing was a gathering of freemen who discussed public matters together. The Thing met once or twice each year.

The Vikings travelled across the globe and left a lasting influence wherever they went

Greenland

Scandinavia

Iceland

North
America

North
Atlantic Ocean

L'Anse
aux
Meadows

Europe

Which parts of the world did the Vikings conquer?

The Vikings travelled across half of the world. They were the first Europeans to discover North America. It is believed that they were there 500 years before Christopher Columbus! They also founded Iceland and sailed to Greenland, Baghdad, Russia, Spain, Italy, Britain, Ireland, France and North Africa.

Leif Ericsson's discovery of North America is celebrated with the raising of this rune stone in his name

Who was Leif the Lucky?

Leif the Lucky, or Leif Ericsson, was a Viking explorer. He was the first European to enter America, in AD 1001. He was the son of another great explorer, Erik the Red.

Is it true that all Vikings were pirates?

All Vikings were not pirates. Most of them were travellers, traders and sailors in search of farmland to settle on. Some Vikings did become fierce pirates and raided towns and looted treasures.

During the second rule of Eric Bloodaxe, silver pennies with a sword pattern on them were issued in his honour

What is the Åby Crucifix?

The Åby Crucifix is one of the earliest representations of the Christian cross. It was crafted by Viking artists in Denmark and symbolised the gradual acceptance of Christianity by Vikings. Made of oak wood and plated with copper, the cross shows Christ as a triumphant king wearing a crown.

The Åby cross is displayed at Copenhagen's National Museum It is almost the same size as the Compsognathus, the world's smallest known dinosaur!

Who was considered to be one of the greatest Viking kings?

King Cnut (Canute) was considered to be one of the greatest Viking rulers. He ruled over Denmark, Norway, England and parts of Sweden.

When did the Vikings start to have kings?

The Vikings were tired of not having a proper governing body. They felt the need for a king who would exercise law and order over their lands. As a result, kings began to make their own laws and governments became more powerful.

What was the Danelaw?

The Danelaw was the name given to those areas of England, which the Vikings seized to set up their own farms. In AD 865, the Great Danish Army invaded England and captured the northern, central and eastern areas of England.

During the raid at the Lindisfarne Priory, the Vikings took treasures from the monastery and some of the monks as slaves. They reportedly threw the others into the sea

When did the first recorded Viking raid take place?

The first known Viking attack took place in AD 793, at a church in Lindisfarne, England. It was the first place in Britain to be raided by Vikings. The first major Viking raid ever was in AD 795, in Ireland.

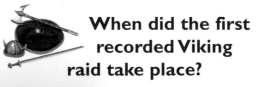

Travel and Navigation

Rough seas, massive warships and savage sailors – these are images that spring to mind when we think of the Vikings. They were not just travellers, but became famous for their long voyages, expert navigation methods and amazing ship-building techniques.

Super Sailors

The Vikings were clever ship-builders. They were amongst the first people to use a keel, or a flat surface on the bottom of a vessel. This allowed ships to cut through the water quickly, even in rough weather.

Tracking Tools

The Vikings were not just good at making sturdy ships. They also kept from getting lost at sea! Viking ships had gold-plated weather vanes on their masts, with an animal figure on top. This figure always pointed away from the direction of the wind, so sailors always knew where to go. They had unusual methods of finding their way around too. Knowing that fleas always move towards the North, the Vikings kept an eye on fleas during voyages, to know which direction to sail in!

The Vikings started crafting bronze weather vanes in the 9th century AD

The clinker design perfected by the Vikings changed the way in which boats and ships were made

What kind of ships did the Vikings build?

The Vikings built long, narrow warships called longships. These were the fastest ships of their time. Longships were also called drakkars (dragon ships) and could be propelled by oars as well as sails.

Most Viking longships were carved out of one piece of oak and their sails were coated with animal fat to make them waterproof!

What was the clinker design?

Viking longships were built with a clinker design – overlapping planks of wood. These planks were fixed together with iron nails. Gaps in between were filled with fur or moss dripped in pine tree tar, to make the ship waterproof! The clinker design gave shape and flexibility to the ship and made it easy to sail in a straight direction.

How did the Vikings travel on land?

When the Vikings were on land, they travelled on horses or horse-drawn sledges. During the snowy winters, they found wooden sledges useful for moving from place to place.

How were Viking ships steered?

Viking ships were steered with the help of a steering board. Also called the rudder or steering oar, this device was fixed on to the right side of the ship with a leather band.

Wooden sledges were a common mode of transport for the Vikings, especially in the icy and snowy winters

Were there many different types of longships?

Viking longships were of many types. The *skula* was a longship with a more rounded shape. The Vikings used it to invade Britain. The *snekkja* was a longboat with 30 oars. However, the most well known longship was one with over 60 oars! It was the largest of all Viking drakkars.

Where on the ship did Viking warriors and oarsmen sit?

Viking longships did not have any seating for its passengers! Trunks and chests, for which there was no storage space, served as seats for both oarsmen and warriors. In this way, the Vikings not only managed to keep their luggage onboard, but also provided seats for themselves!

Why were dragonships useful?

Dragonships were really useful for Viking raids, because they were lightweight and fast on the move. They could be pulled ashore quite effortlessly by hand and allowed for a quick escape. Longships could also sail just as easily on both rough and shallow waters.

FACT BOX

■ Viking longships had special racks along their sides for warriors to keep their shields on. Shield racks made it easy for the warriors to pull out their shields at any time during a battle!

■ The sails of Viking ships were often coloured bright red, like blood, to symbolise the threat of a Viking raid and scare enemy ships!

■ During the day, sailors used a tool called the sun board. It worked like a solar clock, measuring the height of the sun at different times of the day and navigating ships in the right direction. The Vikings also sailed with the help of the stars, the direction of the wind and familiar landmarks.

The clever Vikings used the sun compass, or sun board, to measure the height of the sun, from which they could calculate the distance between north and south

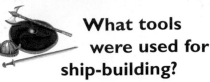

How did the Vikings drill holes into planks of wood?

The Vikings used a drill for making holes in wood. The drill was pressed down on its target from the top by the carpenter and a set of handles was turned at the same time.

T-shaped drills like these were used by Viking carpenters to bore holes into wood

What tools were used for ship-building?

Viking ship-builders used a variety of tools to make their ships. Most of them were quite similar to modern tools, such as hammers, axes and knives. They also used bark spades, sideaxes and drills.

Did the Vikings use any other sailing vessels?

Besides their favourite dragonships, the Vikings used other sailing vessels too. They used ships called *knorrs* for trading and transporting goods. They also had smaller rowing boats for fishing and ferrying people.

How were Viking ships decorated?

Viking ships were sometimes decorated with carved patterns along their sides. Vikings used the *skjøver*, a tool used for creating decorative patterns on boards of wood.

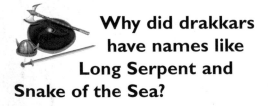

Why did drakkars have names like Long Serpent and Snake of the Sea?

The Vikings named their longships after the fierce animal figureheads that they carved on the front of their ships. They believed that the heads of dragons rand other creatures protected them against the evil spirits of the oceans.

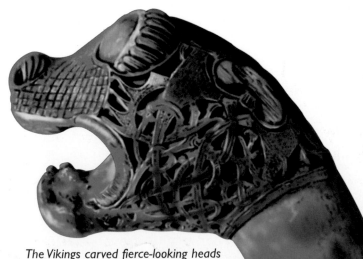

The Vikings carved fierce-looking heads of monsters at the front of their warships to show their enemies that they were ready for a savage fight!

Warriors and Weapons

Battles and bravery were most important to the Vikings. They were warriors who fought fearlessly, for the honour and triumph of their king or lord meant everything to them.

Fighting Force

At first, the Vikings fought mainly on land. They went to the battleground on foot, as they did not have big, strong horses to ride on. The biggest Viking armies consisted of up to 7000 men! Later, the Vikings became masters of sea combat with their gigantic longships and sailing techniques. From small duels and gang raids to grand-scale wars, the Vikings were always ready for combat!

Gearing Up For Glory

The Vikings went to war armed with all kinds of weapons. Wearing helmets of leather or metal, they carried big shields and sharp swords. Dressed from head to toe in bright and protective gear, they would set off in search of wealth and victory!

Although most people believe that the Vikings wore horned helmets, this is not at all true! Viking warriors wore helmets without horns and carried weapons that they sometimes named after giantesses and women warriors

Did Viking warriors wear uniforms?

Viking warriors did not wear any particular uniform. They were expected to choose and arrange for their own clothes before going out to battle.

Who was the most important warrior among the Vikings?

The chieftain was the most important of all Viking warriors. Though many of them could not read or write, chieftains were very powerful, because they were leaders of their army as well as landowners. They travelled to different lands to carry out raids and became wealthy.

Viking warriors sometimes volunteered their services to royal armies known as lid, where they fought in overseas wars or in neighbouring countries

Which piece of Viking armour was made by linking rings of iron together?

Viking warriors often wore long tunics called byrnies or chain-mail shirts. These were over-shirts that took long hours and a lot of money to make. Because they were expensive, they were probably worn only by leaders. Chain mails were also sometimes attached to the back of Viking helmets to protect the neck.

Did the Vikings destroy enemy ships?

The Vikings did not destroy enemy ships, but captured them instead. They believed that ships were valuable, because of the time, money and effort involved in ship-building.

Did the Vikings use bows and arrows?

The Vikings often used bows and arrows for both land and sea battles

The Vikings used bows and arrows for fighting battles and hunting. The bows were usually made of elm wood, while arrows of wood and bird feathers had sharp heads of bone, antlers or iron.

Were Viking sea battles very common?

Battles at sea were not common during the Viking Age. Viking warriors rarely fought at sea and even these battles usually took place close to the shore. They lined up their ships and fired at their target, before boarding the enemy ship and raiding it!

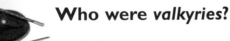

Who were *valkyries*?

Valkyries were warrior daughters of the Viking god, Odin. It was thought that *valkyries* controlled battles and chose which warriors were to die in battle. Vikings believed that *valkyries* took the souls of dead warriors back to Odin's banquet hall, where they were made members of Odin's priviledged army of heroes. The *valkyries* then served them beer and mead in horn-shaped cups.

Warriors could become chieftains if they were from military or noble families. Ordinary men could become chieftains too, if they were skilled with weapons and fighting tactics

The traditional Viking beasts of battle represented victory, feeding on the bodies of those who were slaughtered by Viking warriors!

Who were the berserkers?

The berserkers were Viking warriors who went berserk with rage during battles! The word 'berserk' means 'without shirt'. The berserkers were said to be so charged up that they did not wear protective clothing while fighting, ignored pains and wounds and bit into the sides of their shields!

Which was the most common Viking weapon?

The most common Viking weapon was the spear. The blades of these spears were of many types – long, short, narrow or wide. Some warriors were known to thrust two spears at the same time, with both hands!

What was the *shieldburg*?

The *shieldburg* was a popular defence tactic used by the Vikings. The youngest warriors lined up together with their shields overlapping one another. The line of shields formed a wall to protect the chieftain and senior warriors, who stood behind the young warriors.

What kind of shields did the Vikings use?

Viking shields were usually round and colourful. They were made of wooden boards covered in leather and had a border of leather or metal. A hole in the shield's centre was made for an iron grip.

The word 'berserk' came from the most feared members of the Viking army – the berserkers!

Were there any women warriors during the Viking Age?

There were some women warriors in the Viking Age. They helped their brothers or fathers by joining in raids. Freydis, Leif the Lucky's sister, led a group of warriors and defeated her two other brothers for Leif and herself. She was known to kill women with her axe!

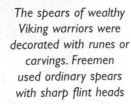

The spears of wealthy Viking warriors were decorated with runes or carvings. Freemen used ordinary spears with sharp flint heads

Society and Daily Life

Everyday life in Viking society was quite simple. During the day, the Vikings went about their daily chores. Merchants travelled with their goods and wares. Farmers worked on the fields with their tools and animals.

Kings, Nobles and Freemen

Viking communities were ruled by kings. Below them were the chieftains, many of whom had their own armies. They formed the *jarl*, or the upper class of Viking society. Next came the traders, farmers and craftsmen, who were known as the *bondi*, or freemen.

At the lowest rung of the social ladder were the *thralls* (*praells*) or slaves. With very few rights, they could be traded like animals and goods. They were not allowed to carry any weapons. Every chieftain had about 12 slaves under him! Most slaves were captured during raids. However, some became slaves because they were born into slave families. Criminals and people who did not pay their debts were also often punished by slavery.

Thralls had no rights or freedom, but they could win freedom by showing loyalty to their owners or by performing acts of bravery

How did the Vikings iron their clothes?

The Vikings used smoothing boards and stones to press out the wrinkles on their clothes. They placed the piece of clothing on a flat board, usually made of animal bone and then ran a small stone over the cloth to iron it out!

Viking women used smoothing boards and glass stones to iron clothes

What kind of work did Viking women do?

Viking women managed the household and farm all by themselves when the men were away. Besides cooking and cleaning, they milked the cows and made dairy products like cheese and butter. They also wove clothes for everyone at home.

The longhouse was the largest house on a Viking farm. It was the centre of all activity, both indoors and outdoors. Inside, the women spun threads, wove clothes and cooked food. Outside, there was place for storing boats, farming tools and animal pens

What was the most common daily occupation of the Vikings?

Farming was the most important occupation of the Vikings. They relied on farming for food and clothes. Most Vikings were farmers as well as raiders, hunters and sailors!

Were there many rooms inside a typical Viking home?

Common Viking houses usually had just one room. All household activities, from cooking to spinning, took place here.

How did the Vikings pay for the goods they bought?

The Vikings did not buy things with coins and notes. Instead, they used broken pieces of silver coins and jewellery, or hack silver. Goods were weighed against bits of hack silver to determine their value. Viking merchants carried a small weighing scale with iron weights of varied values wherever they went.

Viking traders carried bronze scales and silver or metal weights to measure the value of goods

How did most Vikings live?

Vikings typically lived in small farming settlements, near or along a river or lake. Most farmhouses were built with a main hall that stretched across the whole length of the house. Other rooms attached to this hall included the dairy and working rooms. Outside, pens for animals and spaces for storing boats, hay carts and food-drying racks were provided. All members of a family would work on the grounds, feeding the farm animals, drying fish, stacking hay and gathering firewood.

What was the animal house?

The animal house was a place on a Viking farm where all animals were kept. Horses, cows, pigs and sheep lived in these, along with stored meat for the family.

Sheep were very important Viking farm animals, not only for meat, but also for wool, which was shaved off with shears like these

Where did the head of a Viking household sit?

In Viking families, the head of the house sat in a special high chair that resembled a throne!

Did the Vikings have farming tools?

Viking farmers used a variety of farming tools and equipment to help them on the farm. They used iron sickle blades for harvesting crops and wooden ploughs with iron cutting blades for ploughing the fields. These were often drawn by oxen or horses.

The seat of the household head – the throne-like high chair!

Were the Vikings active traders?

Viking merchants travelled to different lands for trading goods. They sold crops, honey, amber, wool, leather, fish and iron for silver, silk, jewellery, spices, wine and pottery. They also bought and sold slaves.

Did Viking children go to school?

Viking children did not go to school. They stayed at home and helped with household chores and farming activities. Their parents taught them lessons on history and religion through stories. Boys were taught to fight and girls were trained to cook, weave and make dairy products.

Where did Viking people sleep?

Ordinary Viking families slept on rugs that were laid out on raised platforms along the walls of their single-room huts. Rich and powerful Vikings had decorative wooden beds with feather-filled mattresses to sleep on!

Wealthy Vikings used beds like this aboard a ship. The small-sized bed with curved head-posts was probably designed to save space

Food and Drink

The Vikings cooked and ate different kinds of foods, both during their travels and at home.

Easy Eating

For the Vikings, whatever was easily available was enough! Freshwater fish like cod and herring were favourites. They also ate shellfish, oysters, eels and seaweed! The main course was usually stew. It was boiled in a huge pot with a variety of vegetables and meat that were easily available.

Food and Fun

The evening meal was important to the Vikings for reasons other than food. It was their time to relax after a hard day of work. After supper, they sat and talked to one another, played games, listened to music and enjoyed storytelling sessions!

Pots, Pans and Plates

The Vikings usually ate out of wooden bowls and plates. Skewers were used for spearing and lifting pieces of meat from iron or soapstone cauldrons. The Vikings also used pots and pans of different sizes and shapes – long-handled frying pans, wooden trenchers and special trays for making cheese.

Viking dishes were generally made out of the wood of beech trees. Some storage jars were ceramic, while serving spoons and ladles were usually made of iron

Food and Drink

How did the Vikings bake bread?

The Vikings baked bread at home. They first ground barley, rye or wheat and kneaded the grain into dough, inside loaf-shaped containers. The dough was then put in a large clay oven and left to bake. Sometimes, bread was also baked as round and flat cakes, on flat iron platters over an open fire.

Viking women spent a lot of their time cooking over a hearth in the middle of their house. They cooked meat and vegetable stew and soups in huge kettles, pots or cauldrons

Which kitchen instrument was used for grinding grain?

The Vikings used a quern to grind grains for bread and other food items. The quern was a hand-mill made up of a pair of round stones, one on top of the other. The stone on top was turned with the help of a handle, which was fixed on to its edge. Grains were placed inside a hole in the centre of the stones and the handle was turned to grind them. Ground grain would then appear from the edges where the two stones met.

How did the Vikings cook food?

The Vikings cooked their food in a cauldron that hung over an open fire. Viking homes had a special fireplace just for cooking. The fire on this hearth was known as *máleldr* or 'meal-fire'.

Vikings ground their grain in heavy quern stones

Did the Vikings use cups for drinking?

The Vikings did not drink from cups. Rather, they drank out of hollowed-out animal horns. Sometimes, they made drinking horns out of metal or wood too. Well-to-do Vikings had elaborately carved metal horns, while the poorest managed with plain horns or wooden mugs.

The drinking horns of wealthy Vikings had special stands to rest on so that the drink did not have to be finished in one go!

Where did the Vikings get their meat from?

The Vikings ate the meat of animals that they either hunted or reared on the farm. Cows, sheep, goats, pigs and chickens were common sources of meat. The Vikings also hunted game birds, deer, bears, hares, walruses, whales and wolves! Seals were important for blubber (fat), which was used either for frying food or as an alternative for butter.

Honey was not only a source of sugar for the Vikings. It was also used to preserve fruits and make fruit wine and mead

Which were the common foods eaten by the Vikings?

As seafaring people, the Vikings ate a lot of fish. They also ate meat, bread and eggs.

How many meals did the Vikings usually eat each day?

The Vikings had two meals a day – the *dagmál* (day meal) and the *náttmál* (night meal). The day meal was taken first thing in the morning, before the Vikings went off to work. The night meal was eaten late in the evening, once work for the day was over.

FACT BOX

■ The Vikings did not use forks to eat with. They only had spoons and knives made of wood or animal bone.

■ Porridge was an important part of the Viking diet. It was made from whole or split grains and cooked in water. Porridge that was made especially for feasts was cooked in milk and served with butter!

■ The Vikings did not have any sugar to sweeten their food with. So they commonly used honey as a sweetener and also as an ingredient to make alcoholic drinks with.

Food and Drink

Did the Vikings eat fruits and vegetables?

The Vikings liked to eat vegetables like garlic, onions, cabbages, carrots and peas. They also enjoyed apples and berries.

Cabbages, onions, carrots and peas were some of the popular vegetables. Apples, berries and plums were also great favourites

What did the Vikings do to keep food from going bad?

The Vikings did not have refrigerators and freezers. They had to preserve their food in other ways. To make meat and fish last longer, they smoked them or rubbed them with salt. Fruits and peas were often dried and grain was used up to bake bread or make ale (beer).

What kind of crops did the Vikings grow on their farms?

Farming was difficult in the hilly regions where the Vikings lived. Nevertheless, they managed to grow oats, barley, rye and wheat on their small plots of land.

Barley was commonly grown by the Vikings of Norway, Sweden and Denmark

What did the Vikings drink?

The most common Viking drinks included milk, beer, mead and buttermilk. Beer was brewed at home. Mead, a strong, honey-based drink, was a favourite at feasts and celebrations. The rich could also afford to drink imported wine.

Is it true that Vikings never drank from glasses?

The earliest Viking drinking vessels were said to be conical or funnel-shaped glasses!

Clothing and Grooming

The Vikings believed in looking good! They wore bright and colourful clothes and attractive jewellery and kept themselves tidy and clean.

Neat and Clean

The Vikings were very careful about hygiene and cleanliness. They bathed everyday and washed their hands before meals. Although Vikings were thought to have scraggly and untidy hair, they were really quite particular about hairstyling! Blondes were considered to be very attractive and many young women loved to leave their hair loose. Sometimes they wore their hair in coils, buns or long plaits. Even Viking men often braided their long beards to keep them in place!

Tidy Tools!

The Vikings used a variety of things to keep themselves neat and tidy. Combs, tweezers and scissors were very important to them. They used hand-carved animal bone combs to keep their hair free from dirt and germs. Another remarkable instrument was the earspoon. Vikings used this for 'spooning' out earwax!

Viking women often attached grooming tools to their dress brooches, so that they were always ready at hand!

Did the Vikings carry bags or purses?

Most Viking men had leather pouches to keep money or important articles in. They strung these pouches to their belts, so that they would not have to hold or carry them.

How did Viking men dress?

Viking men wore long shirts and trousers, which were held up with drawstrings. Over this, they wore a sleeved jacket or coat and tied a leather belt around their waist. Socks and leather shoes or boots completed the Viking male outfit.

It was common for Vikings to wear handcrafted leather pouches on their belts for storing items in

Besides wearing bracelets, how else did the Vikings decorate their arms?

The Vikings often wore armlets or arm-rings crafted in gold or silver. Sometimes, the men wore snake-shaped, spiral armlets. Arm-rings were also ornamented with carved patterns or with twisted braids of silver or gold wire.

What materials were Viking clothes made of?

Wool and linen were the two most common materials used. The Vikings made their own clothes and used vegetable dyes to colour them in shades of blue, yellow, red, orange and brown. The wealthy could also afford to wear silk clothes.

The dressing styles of Viking men were more varied than for women. Viking men wore different types of outfits, depending on their jobs and status

How did Viking women dress?

Viking women dressed themselves in a long, linen under-dress that was either pleated or plain. Over this, they wore an apron-like tunic, which was pinned on with a set of decorative brooches. They often wore shawls over these tunics.

Which grooming tool did Viking women often carry?

Viking women often carried tweezers by attaching them to their brooches with a chain. They used these for plucking their eyebrows!

What kind of hairstyles did Viking men sport?

Viking *thralls*, or slaves, usually had very short, cropped hair. Men of a higher rank had hair that came down to their collars or shoulders.

The basic dress of Viking women was a long, linen garment with sleeves. Over this, they wore several other articles of clothing and jewellery

FACT BOX

■ The Vikings sometimes melted Arab coins in order to make jewellery! For beaded ornaments, they heated up broken glass pieces to create differently shaped and coloured beads.

■ Viking women wore make-up on their faces. They used eyeliner and even bleached their hair!

■ Viking men and women wore cloaks around their shoulders to keep warm in the winters. These cloaks were held in place with intricately carved cloak pins.

Viking men used cloak pins to fasten their cloaks to their left shoulder

Did Viking women wear headdresses?

Depending on which region or time period they belonged to, Viking women wore various kinds of headdresses. The Dublin hood (from Ireland) was a rectangle-shaped, woollen hood, with a point at the back of the head. Viking women of York (in England) wore Jorvik hoods. These were more rounded and had drawstrings for tying the hood from under the chin.

Dublin hoods were generally made of wool, while Jorvik hoods were often made of silk and linen

Why were some Viking shoes known as turn shoes?

Turn shoes were Viking shoes that were hand-stitched inside out and later turned over to leave the seams inside. Other Viking shoes had their stitches on the outside.

What kind of jewellery did the Vikings wear?

Viking men and women were very fond of jewellery. They liked to wear bright and pretty necklaces, pendants, rings, brooches and bracelets.

The most widely used metal for crafting jewellery in the Viking Age was silver

What kind of trousers did the Viking men of Russia usually wear?

The Viking men of Russia wore baggy trousers that came up to the calves, instead of being full-length!

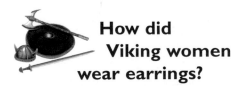

How did Viking women wear earrings?

Though both men and women wore jewellery, only women wore earrings. They attached gold or silver earrings to long chains, which were then looped around the ears!

Religion and Customs

The Vikings were pagans, or people who did not follow Christianity. However, they were very religious people and worshipped many different gods and goddesses. Their beliefs, customs and rituals, too, were mostly based on their religious ideas.

Weddings & Swords

Marriage was an important religious event for the Vikings. Viking marriages were usually fixed by the fathers of the bride and the groom. A bride-price was paid to the girl's family as a payment for marrying her. The girl's father would then give his daughter a dowry, or some amount of money to take to her husband. In Viking weddings, the bride and groom exchanged swords as part of their marriage vows!

Viking swords were named according to the sharpness of their blades or the decorations on their hilts

Comfy with Christianity

The Vikings became comfortable with Christianity over a period of time. They came across the Christian way of life as they raided different communities and settled in various places. Gradually, they adopted the religion of Christianity.

Which Viking god is said to have exchanged one of his eyes for more wisdom?

Odin was considered to be the All-Father, or the ruler of all the gods. Also known as Woden, he was the God of Magic, Poetry and War. According to Norse mythology, Odin swapped one of his eyes in exchange for a drink at the Well of Knowledge, so that he could become even more clever than he already was!

Odin was the ruler of Åsgård, the Viking world of gods and goddesses

What kind of religion did the Vikings follow?

Before they became Christians, the Vikings had their own Norse religion. They believed that there were two forces in the world – gods and goddesses on one side and their enemies, the giants, on the other.

Why were Viking funerals so unusual?

The Vikings believed that when a Viking died, they travelled to another life. For this reason, they often buried the bodies of royal and important people inside a boat or a ship! They would then set the vessel on fire and send it out to sea. Ordinary Vikings were buried in graves, with a few of their belongings. Sometimes, these burial sites were also marked with stones laid out in the shape of a boat.

Did the Vikings believe in heaven?

The Vikings believed that there was only one way to go to heaven – to die in battle. The *Valhalla* (Hall of Heroes) was the Viking heaven, where souls of brave warriors were honoured. The Viking people thought that rainbows led the way to the *Valhalla*.

Born to giants, Loki was Odin's blood brother. This gave him entry into Åsgard and some of Odin's powers too. He often misused these powers and annoyed the Viking gods

Which giant god was punished by Thor?

Loki, the God of Mischief, Tricks and Death, was a giant who did not like the other Viking deities. Legend has it that Loki threw a dart of mistletoe and killed Balder, the God of Light and the son of Odin. Thor punished Loki for what he did.

Were there different burials for Viking women?

Both Viking men and women of rank were buried in ships. Daily items like food, drink, clothes and jewellery were buried with them, so that their soul would have all that it needed in the next life. Women were buried along with household items and jewellery, while men were laid with weapons, tools and even animals!

Who was Thor?

The most popular Viking god was Thor. He was the God of the Sky and Thunderstorms. He was believed to wear a magic belt and gloves made of iron.

The bodies of Viking kings, nobles and chieftains were placed in boats that were buried or set on fire and sailed to sea

FACT BOX

- Some of the days of the week were named after Viking gods! Tuesday came from Tyr, the God of War and Wednesday was named after Woden (Odin). Thursday originated from Thor and Friday came from Odin's wife and the Mother Goddess, Frigga.

- Freyja was the Viking Goddess of Love, Beauty and Fertility. According to mythology, when Freyja wept, she cried tears of gold and amber!

- Thor was always represented with a hammer called the *Mjollnir*, meaning 'the destroyer'. The Vikings often wore pendants in the shape of Thor's Hammer.

In Norse mythology, a strike from Thor's Hammer was powerful enough to kill anyone instantly! No wonder then that the Vikings carried this powerful symbol around as a lucky charm

Which popular saying originated from an old Viking custom?

According to Viking legend, Idunn (Idun) was the Goddess of Immortality and Eternal Youth. She carried golden apples that were eaten by Viking gods when they wanted to become young again. This story is believed to have created the popular saying, "an apple a day keeps the doctor away"!

How were bodies kept from falling off Viking burial ships?

The body was first placed inside a special tomb within the burial ship. The vessel was then covered up with a mound of earth.

The Vikings worshipped in open spaces, where no weapons were allowed

 Why did the Vikings hold three religious festivals each year?

The Vikings believed that their gods wanted something in return for victories at battles and good farming conditions. To offer sacrifices to their gods in gratitude, the Vikings held three feasts each year – *Sigrblot* in summer, *Vetrarblot* after the harvest season and *Jolablot* in winter.

Did the Vikings have temples for their deities?

The Vikings usually worshipped their deities in open spaces. Lakeshores, meadows, hillocks and rocks were considered sacred. At first, the Vikings did not pray in front of any statues. Later, they prayed before carved representations of their deities.

Idunn, the Goddess of Spring and Eternal Youth, was married to a dwarf-god

What was *ausa vatni*?

Ausa vatni was a practice in Viking naming ceremonies. It involved the sprinkling of water over a newborn baby's forehead. The baby was then given a name.

Art and Architecture

The Vikings were good craftsmen and builders. Blacksmiths, goldsmiths, stone-carvers, house-builders and road-layers were all important members of society, because of the specialised work they did.

Home Sweet Home!

Viking builders made stable houses and forts with materials that were easily available. They strengthened walls with strong and closely-fitted wooden planks or logs. At times, they also wove branches of osier (a kind of willow) between the walls for greater stability. The Vikings then plastered these walls with a mixture of animal hair and mud. They constructed smooth floors of packed earth and covered the roofs with grass or wood and straw. Usually, Viking houses did not have any windows!

Creative Craftsmen

The Vikings were just as skilled as artists as they were architects. They specialised in carving and textile weaving. Artisans carved intricate patterns on stones and the walls of their homes and other buildings. They also decorated various articles of furniture with fine carvings.

Viking woodworkers excelled at carving. They carved wavy and knot-like patterns on the walls of churches, houses and furniture too, like this bench at a Swedish church

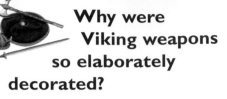

Why were Viking weapons so elaborately decorated?

Weapons were important symbols of wealth and social status. The more ornate a weapon, the richer was its owner! This is why the hilts of swords and daggers were often carved with intricate patterns, inlaid with coloured stones or decorated with silver, copper, gold or bronze wires.

Viking craftsmen often decorated sword hilts with animal heads and curved line patterns, which were then covered with gold and semi-precious stones

Why did Viking houses often burn down?

The Vikings had open fires inside their homes, but they did not have proper chimneys. For this reason, Viking houses were prone to catching fire.

What did the Vikings build to defend themselves?

The Vikings built huge, circular forts of earth, turf and wood as military camps. Within these fortresses were towers, guardhouses and workshops, where weapons were made.

Were there doors and locks in Viking houses?

The doors of Viking houses were wooden, with iron or wooden hinges. They were shut with a latch and locked with a bronze key. Some early Viking houses did not have proper doors, only openings!

In Viking regions where there were fewer trees, stone, instead of wood, was used to build houses

Were the Vikings good at weaving?

The Vikings were expert weavers. Most Viking families had vertical spinning looms in their homes for weaving clothes. They wove clothes in all kinds of patterns and bright colours. Sometimes, gold and silver threads were also used to embroider patterns along the borders of the clothes.

Viking women made clothes on a vertical weaving loom, which saved cloth from being wasted, because it could weave cloth of any width

Did Viking houses vary from region to region?

The Vikings built many different kinds of houses. The typical Viking house was the longhouse, built of wattle, daub, wood and any other material available. In Iceland and other islands nearby, wood was scarce. Here, the Vikings made huts of turf (a mixture of grass, roots and soil) and stone. In Russia, the Vikings used pine logs to build houses.

How did the Vikings make their houses strong and sturdy?

The Vikings placed heavy pillars of wood in a slanted position against the walls of the house. This provided enough support both for the walls and the roof.

FACT BOX

■ The Vikings built houses that had roofs of straw or reed. They added layers of bark from birch trees or the tar of pine trees to waterproof them.

■ The Vikings were masters at stone carving and etched pictures and scenes to tell stories and narrate real life accounts.

■ Bead-working was practised in many towns and cities during the Viking Age. Beads of different sizes, shapes and colours were created from broken glass bottles to make jewellery or decorate clothes.

Beads in the Viking Age were expensive to make. Besides being used in jewellery, they were also the most common items found in Viking graves

Art and Architecture

What is the Jelling style?

The Jelling style is a Viking form of art. It was named after a place in Denmark. The Jelling style is characterised by wavy, ribbon-like patterns of animal figures and abstract designs.

The Jelling style of art, which became popular in the 10th century, was brought to Britain by the Vikings of Scandinavia

How did Viking artists make brooches?

Viking artists usually made brooches with clay or soapstone moulds. The main shape and design of the brooch was cast from patterned moulds. It was then either coated with gold, painted, or decorated with beads.

How many rooms were there in the houses of rich Viking people?

Rich Vikings lived in large houses. These usually had an entrance hall, a kitchen, a main room, a second bedroom and a storage room.

Were the Vikings skilled craftsmen?

The Vikings were skilled craftsmen of wood and iron. Blacksmiths smelted iron to make weapons and tools. Carpenters were experts at carving ships, statues and wooden artefacts. Leather workers, jewellers, goldsmiths and bone workers were also important in Viking society.

Tools for building houses in the Viking Age were similar to modern-day hand tools

What tools did builders use?

The Vikings used a variety of tools for building their houses. Most of these were similar to the ones we use today, such as hammers, chisels and hand drills.

Games and Entertainment

The Vikings held many feasts, some of which lasted for over a week! They had feasts for weddings, religious festivals and even funerals. They also played games and sports to amuse themselves.

Women's Wrestling!

One of the most popular Viking sports was wrestling. Three styles existed – free-style, glima-wrestling and crude wrestling. Glima wrestling was the favourite. It is believed that even the women participated in these matches! Special rules for the sport are said to have been found in the *Grágás*, the Viking book of laws.

The Lewis Chessmen

The Vikings liked peaceful games too. They played board games that were like the modern-day game of chess. We know this because of the Lewis Chessmen, one of the most famous archaeological finds of the Viking Age. The Lewis Chessmen are a set of walrus ivory chess pieces believed to be of Viking origin. Carved sometime between AD 1150-1170, they are considered to be the most complete collection of ancient chess pieces in the world!

The Lewis Chessmen were said to have been discovered by a shepherd in 1831, inside a tiny stone chamber at the edge of a beach

Which Viking musical instrument was sometimes played at story-telling sessions?

Rich people often had story-telling sessions or poetry recitals at home. On such occasions, they called musicians to come and play the harp, or lyre.

 Did they play any outdoor sports?

The Vikings enjoyed a variety of outdoor sports, such as skiing, swimming, wrestling, archery and javelin throwing. Athletic competitions were sometimes held during a feast or a party.

 Which animal featured in a popular Viking sport?

One of the most popular Viking sports was horse-fighting. The Vikings set up competitions between Icelandic horses as a part of feasts or celebrations. It was a serious sport and huge bets were often made on which horse would win.

The Viking lyre was not just played by musicians. It is thought that the instrument was passed around at Viking feasts, so that everyone attending got a chance to play it and entertain the gathering!

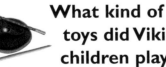 **What kind of toys did Viking children play with?**

Viking children often played with animal figures, boats and weapons made of wood.

 Which Viking sport was said to be like lacrosse?

Knattleikr was a Viking stick-and-ball-game that was very similar to the French game of lacrosse.

How do we know that the Vikings played games and danced for entertainment?

Archaeologists have unearthed several Viking memorial stones, which are carved with scenes of the Vikings playing board games and dancing.

What was *Idrottir*?

Idrottir was the Viking term for all mental and physical exercises. These included gymnastic exercises, like balancing and climbing, or athletic sports like running, jumping and swimming. *Idrottir* also included exercises or sports involving weapons, like fencing and archery. The third category of *Idrottir* involved mental exercises like riddles, mind games and story-telling.

Horse fighting was the most popular form of entertainment for the Vikings of Iceland. Such fights were held regularly, especially after a Thing gathering

Viking bone flutes were usually small, whistle-like instruments made from the thighbone of sheep. However, sometimes the bones of swans and cranes were also used

What was *Hneftafl*?

Hnefatafl, or 'king's table', was a popular Viking board game. Although little is known about it's rules, it is said to have been similar to chess and checkers. Also known as *tafl*, the game involved the use of a wooden or stone board with holes in it and eight game pieces. Each player had to use these pieces to defend his king from the other player.

What kind of materials were Viking board game pieces usually made of?

Game pieces and dice were typically carved out of wood, amber, animal bones or walrus ivory.

Was the panpipe a popular Viking instrument?

Panpipes were played during the Viking Age. Holes of different notes were carved into a single block of wood and then blown into for creating music.

Hnefatafl was a popular Viking board game. It is believed that the game was so competitive that if a player lost a game, they even killed their opponents in anger!

Who were *skalds*?

Skalds were Viking poets and historians who often provided entertainment at feasts by reciting poems and stories. Sometimes they also sang songs.

The Vikings called their ice-skates 'ice-legs'!

Was ice-skating a popular Viking pastime?

The Vikings were fond of ice-skating. They made blades out of animal bone and fastened them on to their leather shoes to make ice-skates.

Did You Know?

Did you know that the Vikings had their own alphabet? They believed that Odin had gifted it to them. They decided to call it the Futhark and the Futhark's letters were called runes. The Futhark was known to have 16 runes.

On Stones and More

Vikings carved their runes with chisels or knives, on stone, wood or bone. They were often painted in bright colours, so that the letters would stand out. Runes were made up of only straight lines, since it is easier to carve straight lines. Runes were also etched into combs, jewellery, weapons and even human skulls!

Uses Galore!

Vikings used their alphabet to write letters and messages, label daily items, keep records and inscribe memorial stones. Fortune-tellers provided horoscopes in runes. The Futhark became a secret language for the few who could read it. Anyone who understood the runes was believed to possess magical powers and wisdom!

The Vikings of Gotland, in Sweden, were very skilled stone carvers. They chiseled out messages and stories in runes and images

Why were Viking coins sometimes split in half?

In the Viking Age, coins were given values according to their weight. If a Viking trader charged half a silver coin for a product, the buyer had to cut the coin into half!

Did the Vikings have any system of punishment?

The Vikings had what they called Ordeals to determine whether someone was guilty of a crime or not. If the person passed these Ordeals, they were considered to be innocent. If they failed, they would be punished as guilty!

Money Breakers – the Vikings had a strange practice of splitting coins for exact payments!

What was the Ordeal By Cake?

The Ordeal By Cake was the name of one of the Viking Ordeals. A special cake was baked for the accused to eat. If he choked on the cake, he was considered to be guilty! If he ate the cake without choking even once, he was allowed to live.

When the Vikings discovered America, why did they name it Vinland?

When the Vikings first came to America, they found many grapes growing there. They knew that grapes were used to make wine, so they called the new land Vinland (Wineland)!

A typical Viking horse collar, decorated with gilded gold and intricate carving

What did the Vikings use to keep horse reins from getting tangled?

The Vikings used horse collars to keep reins from getting tangled. Horse collars were curved, arch-shaped objects that fitted around the horse's neck. The reins were looped through holes in the middle of the collar. Viking horse collars belonging to chieftains and royalty were typically crafted out of leather and decorated with gold or silver threads.

Did the Vikings have toilets in their homes?

The Vikings were thought to have had their toilets outdoors! We know this because of the discovery of a Viking toilet seat in York, England. It was a bench seat with a square hole in its centre. The seat was placed outside, over a smelly hole in the ground!

An early Viking bench toilet, out in the open!

Which popular song is said to have originated from a Viking battle?

The famous song, 'London Bridge is Falling Down' is said to have come from a Viking battle! Legend has it that Viking warriors once destroyed the Bridge in order to move further ahead along the River Thames!

The Ayjershjelmet – a symbol of sure safety and victory for Viking warriors

43

Did You Know?

What was the *Danegeld*?

In AD 865, the Vikings demanded *Danegeld* for the very first time. *Danegeld* was the demand for money or payment in return for peace. If the person who was asked to pay up did not do so, the Vikings would kill them!

Did the Vikings bathe regularly?

It is believed that the Vikings bathed once a week, on Saturdays! They had bathhouses or saunas next to their longhouses for this purpose.

Were runes similar to the Roman alphabet?

The Viking runes were more than just letters of the Norse alphabet. They were different from the Roman (English) alphabet, because each rune had a special meaning behind it.

Each Viking rune had special significance and meaning

What was unusual about Viking skiers in Sweden?

The Viking skiers of Sweden were known to wear a ski only on one leg!

Flints and stones were amongst the first tools for starting fires in the Viking Age

How did the Vikings light fires?

There were no matches during the Viking Age. The Vikings used striking stones to light fires instead. These were pieces of stone and metal that were struck together to create enough heat and, finally, spark, to light firewood!